MW01269290

Made in United States
Troutdale, OR
08/01/2023

11725712R00076